Our Hands a Hollow Bowl

Our Hands a Hollow Bowl

poems

Sharron Singleton

GRAYSON BOOKS
West Hartford, CT
graysonbooks.com

Our Hands a Hollow Bowl
copyright © 2018, Sharron Singleton
Library of Congress Control Number: 2017963715
published by Grayson Books
West Hartford, CT
printed in the USA

ISBN: 978-0-9982588-8-1

Interior & Cover Design: Cindy Mercier
Cover Photograph: Richard O. Singleton
Author photo courtesy of Richard O. Singleton

To all my beloveds, especially Richard

Acknowledgments

Thanks to the following publications for first publishing these poems, some of which originally had different titles.

After Hours: Love Song, I Pledge Allegiance
Agni: Three
Atlanta Review: Write A Poem They Say
The Connecticut River Review: How Everything Longs For its Source or What the Rain Said to the Pearl Necklace; The Milky Way Sends a Message to My Friend Who is Dying
Cream City Review: Livingston County Fair
Diner: What is Left
Ellipsis: And the Two Shall Become...
Grey Sparrow: A Friday in June
The Ledge: To Eat
The MacGuffin: Winter Lullaby; Swallowed; A Long Marriage; Like A Scrap of Michigan Sky; Archeology; Dostoyevsky and the Buddha; This Long Novitiate; Kaiser-Frazer Folds in Detroit
Many Mountains Moving: Stone from Empire Beach, Lake Michigan
Parabola Magazine: I Praise Unsalted Butter
Poetry Quarterly: To the Second Baseman on the Softball Diamond Near My House
Rattle: Ice Fishing
Richmond Magazine: Unfastened; A Thin Thread of Water; With My Daughter and Granddaughter at the Korean Spa in a Strip Mall North of Seattle
SixFold: The Dock-Sitters; Waiting in Line After Christmas; We Sail at Night
Snowy Egret: Christmas Again and Still at War
Terminus: Long Lost
The Sow's Ear Poetry Review: Stone from Empire Beach, Lake Michigan
The South Dakota Review: Western Red Cedar
The Spoon River Poetry Review: What Burns But Does Not Consume
Tulane Review: To All the Dead Fathers
The Wisconsin Review: To All the Dead Fathers

Several poems in this collection were first published in the chapbook: *A Thin Thread of Water*, published in 2010 by Finishing Line Press.

Contents

I
Preparing to Move for the Last Time ... 13
Love Song ... 14
The News Ends with the Body Count ... 15
Christmas Again and Still at War ... 16
Failing to Comfort a Friend Who is Dying ... 17
Not Saved ... 18
How Everything Longs for its Source or
    What the Rain Said to the Pearl Necklace ... 19
Skinny Dipping ... 20
Like a Scrap of Michigan Sky ... 21
Where the Plow Stopped ... 22
This Long Novitiate ... 23
Seed ... 24
So Eden Sank to Grief ... 25
Livingston County Fair ... 26
Wild ... 27

II
Leached ... 31
The Long Way Home ... 32
Thanksgiving ... 33
A Friday in June ... 34
Archeology ... 35
What Burns but Does Not Consume ... 36
Laid Off ... 37
To Eat ... 38
A Thin Thread of Water ... 40
Why I Don't Write Poems about My Father ... 41
Not Too Loud ... 42
Ice Fishing ... 43
Write a Poem They Say ... 45
To All the Dead Fathers ... 46

Unfastened	48
With My Daughter and Granddaughter at the Korean Spa	
in a Strip Mall North of Seattle	49
My Son the Father	50
A Long Marriage	51
Hottest Summer on Record	52
Western Red Cedar	53
Winter Lullaby	54
And the Two Shall Become…	55
We Sail at Night	56

III

Waiting in Line After Christmas	59
What is Left	60
Long Lost	62
Stone from Empire Beach, Lake Michigan	63
To the Dock Sitters	65
Three	66
Descant	67
Who Wouldn't	68
Hyla Crucifer	70
Hymn	71
To the Second Baseman on the Softball Diamond Near My House	72
End of Winter	73
I Praise Unsalted Butter	74
I Pledge Allegiance	75
Swallowed	76
Dostoyevsky and the Buddha	77
About the Author	78

I

We must be still and still moving
Into another intensity

T. S. Eliot, Four Quartets

Preparing to Move for the Last Time

The swing which threw off my children years ago
now hangs sullenly over long sunlit grass,
shifts a loose shoulder when shoved by the wind.

On the porch the cushions of the wicker chair
scroll *finis* in a faded hieroglyph of flowers
as we prepare to move for the last time.

Our narrative in this house has shrunk to the pear on the sill
sinking into its own grainy center and the wasp stuttering
her demise against the window.

But if I follow that trail of scuffed grass backward in time
I see a glimmer, a benevolence, something which holds open
the gates of then and now, something signaling a revival—

like the born-again snake who crawled out of its skin
at the edge of the woods and emerged, parasites gone.
Everything bears its own end and beginning.

When my mother died, I felt her last faint exhalation,
a small summation as the family wept their Aves
and I remembered the bread she made rising

from pockets of air, absence becoming body which then
becomes absent in the eating of it and how all the coming
and going blur into one holy thing, the enfleshed

and always too soon the unfleshing.

Love Song

A roan horse up to his hocks in deepening drifts
stands stone still near the open door of a red barn,
his heavy muscled neck bent, thick fall of snow
collecting in his rough coat. He lifts his great head

and looks at me through the growing dark.
In his liquid eyes I see a litany of seasons—
the colt's delicate ankles, sweat-slicked withers,
glossy rump, and now horse and barn streaked with age.

Robed in silence and snow we stand together, growing
closer or more distant—I can't tell, and through
the veil that falls over this winter evening, we sing
to each other the long song of the decades.

The News Ends with the Body Count

Into and out of my dreams birds fly—
my breath, a ribbon in their beaks rising
and falling. Who has not lain like an effigy,
bright busy self of yesterday encased
in sleep's vault? Who among us, awake
in the dead of night, has not heard
the voice which says, *why live?*

Like silver chisels the first notes
of birds break me open as night relents—
black to gray to opaline blue. Once

we were that which flies, stepping off
into blue arenas, regions of light. Once
a belief in wings whistled through
the hollow bones of our bodies.

Christmas Again and Still at War

This morning a red-tailed hawk
brought down a sparrow in flight

to the feeder. I watched him tear
at the small brown lump until

just a puff of feathers remained,
a bloom of pink on the snow.

At the end of the day,
shadows lilac with dusk, I shuffle,

hooded and muffled against
the cold, eyes tearing with wind,

winter's exhalation caught in snowy
peaks against fences, hillocks of grass,

      and what I want
is a vast mothering snow, the falling

mercy of it, weight and ballast,
swaddling what is rent and disfigured,

journeys blocked, plans undone,
an immense utterance of *no*.

        Let it fall
without ceasing and in backyards,

let the small intentions of sparrows
shelter in hemlocks, under cover

of white wait out the failing light.

Failing to Comfort a Friend Who is Dying

Remember how the moon brushed a path
on waves when you walked the beach, remember
how the sea swallowed your footprints in sand,
sand ground from rock, rock hurtled
from a dying star and the shattered radiance
that rains down on you each night. Remember

how the melon seed sank under the burden
of earth, your heel pressing it down.
Remember how it withered, split open
and surrendered its small green light
to rise months later fat and gold as the moon.

Not Saved

Who has not left her body
        for a moment, lost every plodding thought,
                followed the wild cry of geese

to the smudged horizon? I turn back
        to potato peelings in the sink,
                mutable light through the window—

changed; not saved nor even
        wiser, just a circle widening
                in the small pond of self.

How Everything Longs for its Source or What the Rain Said to the Pearl Necklace

I rave against
windows and doors,
haul the ocean
on my back to you
because I've heard
your breath quick
and faint inside
a locked box.

You are naked
and alone, so I skim
fog from mountains,
harvest snow
from Siberian tundra,
carry to you the sea
that once stroked
your tight-lipped shells.

Skinny Dipping

To walk barefoot
in wet grass, feel
the soft lip of air
on cheek, arms,
belly; to sink into
the drift of liquid
silk over bare skin,
is to begin

again—afloat
in amnio, nothing
between our nakedness
and a liquid firmament,
as at the end, nothing
between our flesh
and the sweet lap
of earth.

Like a Scrap of Michigan Sky

snagged on a fence post; hazy,
faded bluegray, the shirt

hung at the edge of the corn field
all my days of passing through

on my way to school or into town
for a newspaper, the mail, a pound

of this or that. It was limp
to begin with and its folds, web-like,

clung more closely to the splintered
knobby post day after day while

its threads frayed, until, if you were to
hold it up, you could see the warp

and weft of the field through it, each
plowed row curving into the distance.

You could see, in spring, the faint green
of sprouts, sere stalks in fall.

In time you would see thistle, ragweed,
marestail, then the bulldozer

and backhoe and soon small
pink and green houses would bloom

from that earth. Now look
through the wicket of your hands

from which the blue shirt has disappeared.
Look at your bent and misshapen fingers,

each knuckle swollen and knob-like,
see how the flesh has shrunk,

skin thin, shiny
and when held to the sun, translucent.

Where the Plow Stopped

I push through furrows of sun-bleached grass, oats,
rye, timothy—old testaments to these abandoned

acres. Wild daisies blouze and goldfinch light fires
in trees. From a honey locust, scabbed and thorny

at field's edge, tiny green worms curl and fall like
good intentions. The hot clover-chamomile scent

of August's ancient scorch fills my nostrils and lungs,
a final harvest in the last rage of summer.

This Long Novitiate

Kneeling in dirt I pull weeds,
toss them on the compost pile—
God-ridden hot heap of waste,
dark genesis of decay. Sun

rakes my hair, licks my neck,
presses me down—inearthed
my roots tendril under leafy mulch,
calcium deposits of fibula,
tibia, femur. Palms wave,

fingers leaf out, open blue holes
in the sky. Solar winds blow
from my plexus, bronchia
branches into coral, lilac veins
a delta's waterway. My hips are

plow blades, equinox, earth's axis
delivering spring, fall. The sap
of words tapped rises in my throat.
Heart, that dark apple quartered,
falls open, cruciform.

Seed

I lay down
life, crave

earth. Time's
bell clangs

death, chimes
birth, folds me

in its grip.
Harrowed

in the grave
I twist. Split-

ting the shell
I leap

from the furrow,
an old god,

green
and knowing.

So Eden Sank to Grief
from *Nothing Gold Can Stay* by Robert Frost

As the gate of summer closes
behind us, not only leaves, degrees
and wormy apples fall but

something within begins to give.
Trees form a ragged border
around the yard, reach out

to each other across the fading
blooms of the small garden.
I wander through vegetable beds

collapsed inward, skeletal plants
yawning and scratching each other
with dried vines. But here, swollen

with sweet and tangy juice, are two
fat red tomatoes held out on
withered arms that poke from cages,

the future secure in gold-tinged seeds,
jubilant and defiant of the dark
and stinging cold that is to come.

Livingston County Fair

What we want are wings,
        or some way to leave.

Tilted and whirled, stars blur
        beneath our feet

as we spin, spill,
        stagger out onto

19th century dust, gloss
        of an old spun

sweetness gilding our faces.
        Across a cricket-thick

field to thin shells of barns,
        our dull fingers

linger, press against
        the immense rippling

mirage of the Percheron.
        At the end, from towers

of light, weightless we fall
        into the hot mouth

of night, bereft
        and beguiled as exiles.

Wild

It is as if the sun had extruded itself,
dripped hot gold of wild mustard
across fields. But to what end?
To raise up what is profligate, pungent,
uninvited and to not care—
to propagate, burn the world's nerves
with its blinding innocence.

*

Pretty as any who are chosen,
black-eyed Susan will not conform,
not stop roaming. Flagrant and careless
she turns her face west, swishes
her yellow skirt across that burnished floor
lights the plains with her velvet gaze.

*

You may drink of chicory,
cut its stubborn stems for your vase.
It will refuse, pale and wilt.
Thin-skinned, blue-eyed ancient,
elbows stiffly crooked, it wants nothing
but to be alone and die
mouth open to the milky sky.

II

...go out of those hours, that house,
the enfolding limbs, go burdened to learn:
you must sing to be found; when found, you must sing.

Li-Young Lee from *The City in Which I Love You*

Leached

As if shackled, we never lifted our eyes to what might
have been over the rise of rutted weedy fields,

yet we rose each morning; ignorant, worn,
weighted by sagging buildings, narrow dirt roads,

by acres of struggle between each farm—
the pale-faced farmer farthest from town,

so poor his boys didn't have underwear; the two girls
who lived together at the edge of the village. But not

girls, large solid women, farm hands, too shy to speak.
They swung hay bales, crouched on stools at 4:00 am,

shot streams of warm milk into galvanized pails;
the one divorcee and two widows who worked the night shift

at the factory, pacing the edge of railroad tracks
on their breaks, taking long drags on cigarettes,

orange tips glowing like tiny searchlights;
my young mother and father trying to patch the ragged

screen door of our lives; the one Indian woman
left on that plain, who lived and died alone in an abandoned

chicken coop, and the permed housewife rousing
from its torpor the wheezing organ in our church,

pumping its pedals until it throbbed and her chins quivered
and sweat broke out on her forehead, until our

quavering voices took flight and rose together like
nameless birds soaring high above leached wheat fields.

The Long Way Home

If, as with a snow globe, you could peer through
a blizzard of flakes you would see my thin shape

trudging across frozen stubbled cornfields, from
the four-room house to the three-room school,

slipping like a bead on a wire, from one narrow world
to the other. Crows follow, scrabble for half-buried

kernels. Pirouetting up from frozen furrows
their ragged wings carve air, harbingers

with rusty-hinge voices, they shriek my then into now.

Thanksgiving

There is the cabin paneled in knotty-pine,
the four of them at the table. See how
the yellow light sulfurs the air, gilds their hair
as they turn to and away from one another—

kitchen so small the mother can barely
squeeze around chairs to serve. 1952
and it is her idea to walk by the lake
after dinner—a normal family.

Dusk and the world has withdrawn,
happy confusion of other families concealed
in the glow behind curtains. But peer
into the stillness of their winter, at flakes

that seem shaken within a globe,
dome that might shatter at the lightest
tap. Note how the skeletal
stalks of weeds rise out of snow, bent

like bones of the famished. Now fissures
begin to spread across the frozen surface
of the father's silence, each ice crystal
that melts on their blind faces—a gift.

Watch as they move further away around
the curve of the lake, disappear
in their last walk together
as if into safety.

A Friday in June

I collected my trowel, shovel and rake, drove to my mother's,
stopping at a nursery to buy topsoil and compost to renew
her flower beds. All day I planted impatiens, begonias, geraniums,

mixing new earth with the sandy old, worried that the house
is too much for her, former dancer, gymnast who now pinches
her mouth shut at the encroachment of spider webs, dust.

Lunch at her picnic table—chicken and mayonnaise on white bread,
iced tea she held in a hand that shook. Later I drove home through
the green evening, past the pond with the pair of swans trailed by

one surviving cygnet, past the sagging farm house almost obscured
by old lilacs, fallow knolls of meadow, the lights of a small carnival's
ferris wheel blinking against a pearled sky, past a giant balloon gorilla

gracefully waving its blue arms over used cars and finally into
my driveway, where the teen-age boy from across the street
was shooting hoops under the street light, dodging and weaving

between imagined opponents, his long thin body leaping for the shot
and still in my mind's eye, his right hand and wrist curve over
where the ball once was, his left hand, palm up, cups absence.

Archeology

At fifteen I wanted perfect, not those silent
choked winters, the long simmer of evenings,
my father behind the newspaper, only
his factory-scarred, nicotine-stained hands visible.

One night he showed me his work, held out
on his palm three small steel ball bearings.
In the kitchen light, they glinted bright and hard
as the face of my contempt. He dropped them

into the pocket of his work pants. The loss
of that evening was not a gift not offered
but a gift refused. I wish I had one now
to lie in a dish on my dresser, to warm in my hand,

as smooth and perfect as the long-buried bone
of one so silent and still unknown.

What Burns but Does Not Consume

When the small lion cub on TV
staggered under the rough tongue

of the lioness I knew my mother and myself.
Strong, blond and charged, the friction

of her energy, combustible as struck flint,
smoked through our lives. She irons,

smacks the iron down. The board, covered
with scorch marks quivers under the assault,

the shirt gives up. Heads of flowers flinch
as she walks by, petals bruise under her caress.

Jars of beans, corn, pickles march in tight formation
on shelves in the cellar. Under her foot

the pedal of the old Singer groans
as my flour sack dresses fly from her hands.

Evenings in the steamy kitchen, faint smell
of burnt potatoes, she stands radiating

heat at my back. I hold the edge of the table,
my skinny eight-year-old legs braced against

the force of the brush, my head is yanked back
with each stroke, snaps forward, is yanked back.

I am kindling to her flame as the fine strands
of my hair rise up like a bonfire.

Laid Off

My father drives the rusted Chevy along empty rutted roads.
He is sober. We don't speak. My mother is at work in a small factory,
sewing canvas tarps and has sent us deep into the country to buy
a second-hand freezer. Bleak and weather-beaten, the farmhouse rears up
in furrowed November fields like a ship adrift in heavy seas. The woman,

thin as winter light, in muddy boots, dirty apron, hair scraped back,
stands in the bare yard. My father pays the woman forty dollars,
his face etched like a woodcut. I shiver and whine about the cold until
she silences me with deepwater eyes and, with grave courtesy, asks,
What will you do when winter really comes?

To Eat

Tonight I will bring dinner to my mother
who is dying of cancer—

a light pasta dish, salad, cherry pie.
She'll try but she won't eat. And yet

she still wants to cook. Nauseous, weak,
almost blind, she stands over the stove

turning out sauerkraut and spareribs,
vegetable soup, apricot muffins.

She tastes only a mouthful, the rest
is given away or goes in the bulging freezer

as her own flesh diminishes, host
to a devouring bloom of cells.

In the garage, large tins of flour,
racks stacked with pasta, enough to last

through any calamity and beyond,
even shelves in the linen closet converted

to hold soups, juices, jellos, crackers.
She shakes her head at herself but

little piles of clipped recipes, grocery lists
still clutter tables. Her words thin to bone,

frut, bak sod, crem—food, her tether
to earth just holding. We have arrived

at the last of life's reversals, that double-
edged verb, *to eat*, being conjugated

by her own body. Soon, I will commit
the indignity of clearing out her house—

but it's the freezer I dread,
shutting off its hum, uncovering layers

of homemade soups, cakes, mounds
of frozen meat buried deep, until I reach

the bottom, the empty cavity stained,
sticky with crumbs, juices that ran.

A Thin Thread of Water

After the war was over, after
the factory closed,
my father took any odd job he could find—
swung an axe on a trestle
of the Grand Trunk line,
once nearly severing his thumb.
I used to trace the red raised scar,
crooked like a train derailed—
it seemed a wound from some kind of war.

After that he cut and baled hay on McKenzie's farm,
brought home eggs, unplucked chickens, payment
we didn't despise.
I sometimes saw him through a haze
of tawny dust, smaller in the distance,
bent under the heavy arm of the sun.

Years later, in the parking lot of Montgomery Ward,
I look west where streets slope
to a shallow valley then rise again
and think of the summer
he pried boulders
from the river that ran there—
so they could bury it, so commerce
could sink its pillars in the riverbed

and I wonder if,
now bereft of sun, air,
stick boats of children, if
deep under my feet
a thin thread of water
still bends around rocks
relentless.

Why I Don't Write Poems About My Father

Old, mottled, algaed
and scarred where hooks
have ripped, the fish
has gone deep,
has descended through brown-
gold pillars of water,
as if through a temple ruin,
down beyond the reach
of light, to lie hidden
among weeds—tattered fins
and fronds tremulous
with the lake's slow
breathing—the only sign
of the fish's presence,
a shivery circle, unnoticed
except by the heron
and fisherman.

Well hooked by his quarry,
the fisherman wants
to catch and not catch,
to scrape away
the armor of scales,
open and gut the creature—
and still glide harmless
upon the wide eye of the lake,
oars dipping, rippling
the surface,
the shadow of the boat
sliding across the shadow
that is the fish.

Not Too Loud

My mother walked to town for groceries,
sat up all night by the coal-burning stove
to make sure the house didn't burn down.

She borrowed my skates, danced by herself
on the ice, picked blackberries alone
in the woods, killed a rattler with a hoe,
even ironed my father's pants when he decided

to leave. When she was dying, the minister
came to comfort, asked her if she was ready.
Not really! she said, and it was clear
he had a nerve to ask. After she died,

I found a notebook with a few words
scribbled in her large round hand—

It's New Years Day. I woke up early,
walked out into the snow, said,
Happy New Year world—but
not too loud.

Ice Fishing

It was never easy—
        my mother's blond German

energy, father's whisky-fueled
        Irish melancholy,

abiding together in the same
        small house

for fifty-six years; the endless,
        almost wordless

battle over the bottle
        and her uncontrollable

cheerfulness.
        The night my father died

my mother struggled
        not to cry, simply said

I loved him.
        Oh, who has words

to speak
        of the winters

of those days when the lake
        was always

frozen, when
        my father built

a shanty, spudded through
        a foot of ice

to sit in the close heated shack
        as if

in the darkness of a heart's
        chamber,

to sink a hook through
        the hole,

the red and white bobber
        floating,

skin of ice already forming.
        I love

that she loved this
        in him

his desire to drop
        a lure

in black water,
        the long-chilled wait,

then to wrench
        from the depths

a gasp of bright living—
        and to let

what could not be hooked
        be unhooked.

Write a Poem They Say

about your mother dying.
A lot of good material there—
grief therapy they say. I write

No, while I coax her
with rice pudding, write *No*
while I make her bed
with silky cotton sheets—
800-count, appeal to doctors
for stronger drugs.

At eighty-eight, she perks up
at the mention of medical marijuana,
thinks it might be fun to try.

                Meanwhile,
a cold alphabet
of sparrows huddles
along the wire.
I am the one on the end,
a little apart, braced
against the wind, gripping
a thin strand of silence.

To All the Dead Fathers

who loved and ruined
their children, fathers
whose bleached shanks
and finger bones,
if laid end to end

would make a thousand
bridges spanning
a thousand oceans
on which the children
could cross in the sweet
amnesiac air.

To my father whose life's
work lay on his palm,
three bright ball bearings—
I name them rage, pity,

love. To the fathers
whose absences were
as hacked limbs.

To all the dead fathers
whose children refused
to be born, ungoverned
as sparrows plucking
seeds from dry grass.

To the dead fathers
who stalk their sons'
and daughters' dreams,
who crouch beside a bed,
trying to remember how

the silken heads felt
beneath their hands,
trying to touch a foot,
wrist, remembering
how small and delicate
the collarbones were

and when they pulled
away, how the grasp
on nothing felt.

Unfastened

When I lifted the heavy rusted iron
in the antique shop I thought
of my grandmother—three children,
heating water, galvanized wash tub,
ribbed scrub board, raw knuckles,
the sizzle of a wet finger testing
the iron, pushing its blunt wedge into
the children's Sunday ruffles and pleats
she has sewn herself, sweat running
between her breasts, under the camisole,
petticoat, corset, the long stockings,
laced-up shoes, limp apron
on gritty, sultry Chicago Saturday nights
and she doesn't know where he is.
She has taken her place in the line
of bound, crimped, laced-up women,
whale bones pressed against their ribs,
the closest they would get to something
wild and loose. She doesn't yet know
she will be tempted to step out of herself,
slip over the rail of the ferry
stitching its way across the gray silk
of Lake Michigan, come unzipped
from her flesh, released from the tight net
of veins, each white knot of bone
finally unfastened.

With My Daughter and Granddaughter at the Korean Spa in a Strip Mall North of Seattle

We undress, stroll into a steamy rain forest
of women—the fifteen-year-old, a sleek reed
pliant in her slight curves, my daughter, forty,

serene and glossy as a yacht, sails ahead,
and I, scarred and pouched, runes of compromise
written on my body, follow. We lower ourselves

into the tiled tub and a long soak at 110 degrees,
not watching but watching every shape and shade
of us slip slowly into the pool—

small pointed breasts uptilted, pendulous bottoms
quivering. We close our eyes, sink into our nakedness,
sigh at the tenderness of water. On tables, we are scrubbed

by smiling Korean women, sweat running down their faces,
muscled arms. Vigorous, business-like,
they lift our arms and legs, swab ears, belly-buttons,

all the crevices, flood buckets of hot water
up and down our bodies washing away dead skin
and grime we didn't know was there. You wish

it would go on forever. Stretched out on the table
next to me, my daughter, creamy and gold,
glistens like an offering to the gods. The women's

warm hands knead, sweep along the length of our bodies,
salve with oils and balm. Soft-lipped, eyes
half-closed, priestesses, we return, stroll through

the door and the men look up from their card game
a little awed and uncertain, reach out to stroke the new silk
of our old selves—all our concessions now cancelled.

My Son the Father

kisses the foot of his child
as the small arch curls in delight.
His fingers curve in benediction around
the boy's silky head—and now the father
begins to understand the rounding of pebble,
plum, egg, span of bow, bridge, this fat
circling earth, even the Buddha's smile,
the whole arc of love, and that in his
hands he holds its best invention.

A Long Marriage

Moles go about their dark business,
in new grass raise tunnels that I stomp down.
Exoskeletons of cicadas cling
to the porch lattice and the wolf spider,
with a huge blue sac of eggs slung
under her belly, can barely move.

At rest from weeding vegetable beds,
I drink iced tea, watch my husband
wrestle the lawn mower back and forth
across the lawn, think of the long muscles
in his back, his tan forearms and strong bare
toes. Soon the heat will drive us in, while
at the end of the row, the rake and hoe
with their once-red handles lean against
each other on the fence. Who can say

what happiness is? It is May—
buds form in folds of broccoli plants,
pea vines sprout small white wings
and tonight outside our bedroom window
the moon will lavish silver on these new hours.

Hottest Summer on Record

there's no
resisting

the heat   the air
sags with moisture

boundaries blur
between sea and sky

both washed
in bluegray congruity

air becomes
ocean and we wade

into it   lungs
open and close

like gills   back
bones   prickle

with   forgotten
fins   each cell

a pouch of   liquid
edges   dissolve

speech   thought
becomes   vapor

spangled   with sweat
your body   slips

into mine   and
fin to fin   we stroke

together   wet briny
nearly boneless

Western Red Cedar

Like stones heavy in a backpack,
we hauled our yammering selves,
threadbare bickerings,
who said what to whom—
into the Olympic Peninsula rain forest.

As in a fairy-tale we came upon
a colossus of a tree, one of only a few
in a million acres still standing.
Furred with acid-green moss, shattered crown
high above the forest, the mad dog centuries
absorbed in its pith, carved into its circle of ribs,
this thousand-year declaration reared up
in the wet green murk. Our own stories
dropped from our mouths like toads.

Looking straight up we staggered
as if drugged. The tree's presence
rang through us like a deep-throated gong,
sounding a silence so deep, for once
we could not hear the sour tongues
of our own desolation.

Winter Lullaby

Every fall a day arrives
sudden and sharp as a blade—
winds from the north
and certain knowledge
of a killing frost that night.

I stop what I'm doing,
rush to the garden
to salvage the last
of the eggplant, peppers,
zucchini, a few leathery
tomatoes. I clip marigolds,
hydrangeas, cut sage,
rosemary, basil as my hands
stain green.

We sink into bed, my body
fragrant with a wild and bitter
perfume and sleep
folded into each other
like new leaves while
night hardens, plants shudder,
blacken, collapse into earth.

And the Two Shall Become...

Your tongue   a spoon
        my hips   a cup   your
fingers dip   my
        back   an arch   my
breast   a dune   our
        legs   a vine   your
root   my bloom   my
        sap   the wine   my
thighs   a stream
        your hands   the oar
my throat   a grape
        your mouth   the fox
my cry   a pearl
        your flesh   the lock.

We Sail at Night

from Newport Light through warm wet air,
sails' bellies just full, the only sound
the shush of water against hull
as we skim the edge of the known world.

The knot meter says our progress is slow,
depth sounder lit with warning. But

behind us in the phosphorus wake
tiny sea creatures follow, the source
of their energy gone, yet still buoyant,
still casting their faint green light.

III

Green was the silence, wet was the light...

Pablo Neruda - Love Sonnet #40

Waiting in Line After Christmas

What if all things could be
exchanged equally—

that is, not money
for things but forgiveness

for a vowel no one has ever
heard before. What if

I gave you dusk from the skin
of a black grape

and you gave me
the desire to tap dance again.

Give me your complete
attention and I'll give you

the scent of rosemary for three
winter nights. Perhaps,

in plain brown wrapping,
the postman will bring you

chimes from the bells courtesans
wore on their ankles if you will

send back six prayers folded
as cranes. There might be

an exchange center so the grief
I gave you for the pain

he gave me might be turned in,
to wait like ice waits for fire, like

stone waits for water, like
never waits for maybe.

What is Left

> *To be without some of the things*
> *you want, a wise man said,*
> *is an indispensable part of happiness.*
>   Stephen Dunn

Have you noticed
        how everything tilts
                toward something—

the telephone pole
        with its cargo
               of voices

leaning toward houses,
        the boy on his bike
                and the thin girl

bending their heads
        to each other
                and of course,

the whole field
        of sunflowers
                arcing from east

to west, a thousand
        dark eyes
                on the sun.

The earth doesn't rest
        on the back of a turtle
                but on the mouth

of desire. And yet
        the balloon always
                escapes the tug

of the child's hand,
        rising until
                the red speck of it

disappears into blue—
        then tears, a reaching
                toward heaven, palms open.

And what the wise man
        didn't say—
                that the other

indispensable part
        of happiness is learning
                to love what is left,

this buckling fence,
        rusty mailbox
                and the slow perfection

of its leaning.

Long Lost

Unlike Michael, the gorilla who painted,
> gave exhibitions and knew sign language,

this gorilla has no language, no paint,
> no press release. He swings

from dead limbs, climbs plaster rocks, pulls
> bananas, lettuce from a blue plastic tub.

This one prowls under artificial sunlight and I don't
> turn away as he scratches, chews.

When his eyes meet mine, I can hold his gaze
> only briefly, embarrassed

under the scrutiny of that flat bloodshot stare—
> as if I have just run into a long-lost

cousin, carrying his poverty like a hot coal.
> Always I come back to his cage, searching

for a way out of my skin, startled by the theology
> in the ape's gesture as, with supple wrist

and delicate forefinger, he reaches toward the bars—
> it is Adam's own as he stretches

to touch God and the moment
> when *in the beginning* begins.

Stone from Empire Beach, Lake Michigan

Smoother and more shapely
        than a rock, which speaks
                with sharp intent,

this sweet weight
        hefted in the hand
                fits curve of palm

like a breast, small loaf,
        a cool thought from water's
                deep intelligence.

Who can know
        the language
                of this ancient

tribe, its former
        speech of stars
                and firmament

hardened by contracting
        earth into one long
                vowel of silence.

Imagine
        its fiery plummet
                through the spark and fuse

of beginning, its slow descent
        into gravity, earth,
                its mottled flesh now

rubbed and tumbled,
        surrendered
                to the muscled

arm of the wave.
        It is enough
                to wash ashore,

  lie racked and cobbled
     among one's neighbors,
        to be ground down

  grain by grain,
     to bleed
        the common colors

  to become every
     footprint
        on every beach.

To the Dock Sitters

To sit on a dock which has walked out
on stiff legs twelve to fifteen feet
from the weedy shore, one board after
another drawing your gaze across
the wide-eyed lake whose color deepens
further out, to sit on this dock
which wants to hold you, even
rock you a little, to dangle your feet,
whiter in the green glassy water, to gaze
into that silent world where minnows eddy
around your toes, where sand allows itself
to be shaped by ripples of water, where
lilies witness to you as that which endures;
to look out on that lake, as birds dip low,
as men in quiet boats cast their lines searching
for what has gone deep and shadowy;
to lie back on gray, splintered, sun-warmed
boards in the silence of light—is to allow

that tight band constricting your breath
to loosen, is to quench your thirst for
the present. To sit on such a dock is one
of the forgotten beatitudes—blessed
are you, dock-sitter, for you shall be
shriven, your humor restored
and your pant legs cool and damp.

Three

Two is just this and that
while three is a way out.
Two stutters, clicks shut,
begins and ends with itself.
Three strains toward the unknown,
is an arch, an angle, a reaching.

Two roses in a vase on a sill
and, lizard-like, your blood cools,
eyelids flutter, almost close—
three and you begin to consider
a different job, a trip to Brussels
or, standing at the window, think:

> I'll dig a pond in the middle
> of the lawn, add goldfish
> and frogs, a painted turtle,
> water lilies with cupped white flowers—
> birds will drink, maybe a heron. See how she breaks
>
> from the shallows, opens
> the blue fan of her wings, rises
> over the tree line, see how the water
> quakes with her leaving.

Descant

        Swift fallings and risings

outside the kitchen window.

        Angles, curves,

   hieroglyphics

old as air,   beyond

        translation—
              incantations

from branch
     to branch—

           jays, juncos,

finches, wrens—

       cascading song

            overflowing

   the small
       feathered vessel.

Who Wouldn't

Seventeen years
underground,

a long slow climb
through black earth,

then into the light,
a kaleidoscope

of red, yellow
and green, the sun

a god—none
of which

the cicada knew
existed. Who

wouldn't leap
from that dank

tunnel, break out
of stiff armor,

soft body eager
to enter or be

entered. Who
wouldn't fly

to the tops
of trees, sing

until the world
was deafened

by urgency,
that long shrill

wail, decibels
rising and falling

as new nymphs
drop from trees,

litter the ground
with empty husks,

twist down into
the earth's body.

Who wouldn't want
to practice

resurrection, discover
another nativity.

Hyla Crucifer

*Latin name for the spring peeper because
it carries the mark of a cross on its back.*

Black robes flapping,
    three crows descend
        on the bare tree,

shout law   law law!
    In the deep Easter
        of the marsh

a chorus of spring peepers
    hollers mercy, tuck
        eggs in leafy muck.

Hymn

Crouched in a font of pale dust
a new church in raw suburb
points its sharp finger at the sky.

Inside hymns and prayers erupt
from our throats like startled birds,
beat against walls and windows while

across the road in abandoned pastures
the faint hosannas of wild grass,
those ten thousand tribes

which rise up and bow down.

To the Second Baseman on the Softball Diamond Near My House

You forget everything else on this evening
in late summer—bills you haven't paid, the argument
you had with your brother, the one who will be
in your bed tonight, as you smack your fist
into the hollow of the oiled and sweat-stained glove.
You hunch a few feet from second base, forearms
on your thighs, your body loose and potent.

Your girlfriend watches, lolls on soft worn grass,
cheers you on in your smallest victory. The music
of our voices lifts with every runner tagged out,
every ball lobbed across the plate for a strike,
with every ball hit high and arcing almost
out of sight into the blinding lights
of an everlasting now. We have stepped out

of time's river as *Hey, batter, batter—*
echoes across dusty playing fields in other cities
and other years. You haven't started to drink
too much, don't yet know about dark shadows
on x-rays and the divorce is still years off.
It is you I think of when I pray the old prayer—
shield the joyous, pity the afflicted.

Let us remember this evening as if it is
pressed between squares of glass, wings
stilled and fixed in flight.

End of Winter

A silver maple stepped out of fog this morning,
shook her limbs free of ice-sequins
as scudding come-along clouds shredded themselves
against the pink horizon. The world
is on the move again. Yesterday morning

I had a call from a friend out of touch
for thirty years and in the afternoon
found my lost ring in the hem of a curtain.
Last night my dead father offered his hand
in a dream and I, scalded by years of his not-touching,

took it. Now outside the kitchen window, from the end
of each sagging branch, the old Blue Spruce
sends out shocking green fingers. The thawing earth
is casting off its winter shroud as sparrows whirl
and polka-dot the swirling skirt of sky.

I Praise Unsalted Butter

it is cheap for the price
and also pearl buttons which keep
secrets, translucent parings
from babies' fingernails.
And the danger of color—dare
to enter the tabernacle of delphinium;
I will wait at its threshold to see
your transfiguration. And this is just
here and now. What about
the Assyrians, their white colts
and amber bracelets, the frogs
that rained down on Leicester,
Massachusetts in 1953. What about
nipples and contrails, gold lamé,
branching dendrites you will
never see. What about that bright
planet that does a little jig
when you look at it. Yes, I know
there's more. There will always be
the thin Vietnamese girl, arms
flung out, running naked down
the world. She has swallowed
language, left us with
a shriveled tongue. So we
hold up earthy mercies; spores
and otter dung, kaleidoscopes
and saliva, Fritz Nielsen, a bearded man
who spends his time in tops of trees
in the Amazonian rain forest.
They all want in—freckles,
the Sangre de Christo mountains,
burnt sugar, the tall Maasi woman
who yelled at me, pale honey-colored
toes of mice. And as cherished
by Tibetan monks as gold dust,
here are tightly folded purple ruffles
of rhubarb. They close with a piercing but
open with the spirit's breath.

I Pledge Allegiance

to the earth because the awk! awk! awk!
of the pileated woodpecker peels back
the cataract of night from the eye of this day,

because, with long sinewy hands, clouds
stoke Big Bluestem prairie grass, because
the blue whale sings her song in purpleblack waters.

I pledge allegiance to the rain who wrings his hair
over all our gardens and the wind frothing
her skirts, to the sizzle of yellow finch,

for which I stand, for the nation's blue and white
stars winking in the galaxy of hydrangea. I pledge
allegiance to what quakes, the long groan of rockbone

splitting open, to the volcano's burning tongue
sucking green from blackened earth
and to the holy hunger of the vulture. I pledge

allegiance to our one life under all the gods,
to the mute worm who parts the earth and, in time,
brings freedom and justice to all.

Swallowed

After Hal Borland, former nature writer for the New York Times

This Hunger Moon, unearthly bright
on the snow below, is polished steel,
its light as cold as ice-vapored breath.

Lifeless sun, it doesn't burn yet casts
on white ground charred skeletons
of black-boned trees. Tall candles of cedars
flare and pines on the hill brush wingtips

across frozen earth. Glyph-like footprints
are scribbled in hollows where the fox prowls,
the green light of her eyes the only stars.

It was her wail of hunger that woke me
and the rabbit's one shriek before
its conversion. I want not to have
heard it, want the morphine of sleep

under this surgical moon but the night
is brutal with beauty—the throat
that has already swallowed us.

Dostoyevsky and the Buddha

The World Will Be Saved by Beauty
Dostoyevsky
I was born into the world ... for the salvation of the world
Buddha

Perhaps we'll be saved
by the beauty
in what is lacking
as emptiness
makes of our hands
a hollow bowl

or by the beauty
of the unsaid—
the note blown across
the mouth
of the empty bottle

by what is reduced
and waiting—
broth boiled down
to its hoard of gold

by all that is about
to be—

and suspended from the tap,
the drop
that swells with light
before it falls.

About the Author

Sharron Singleton was born in Chicago and raised in rural Michigan when it was still mostly farming country. Before she began writing poetry she was a social worker serving low-income families and the mentally ill, and she worked as a community organizer around issues of civil rights and the anti-nuclear war movement.

She won the James River Writers Contest in 2009 and was named Poet of 2010 by the journal *Passager*. She has won many prizes for her poetry. Ms. Singleton's chapbook, *A Thin Thread of Water*, was published in 2010 by Finishing Line Press. She has taught poetry in Scottsville and in Charlottesville, Virginia at WriterHouse, and until recently was the Poetry Editor of *Streetlight Magazine*.

Sharron Singleton says, "I have been married for 57 years, have two children, five grandchildren and a great-grandchild. Oddly I sometimes feel younger now, and certainly freer, than I did when I was nineteen."

www.ingramcontent.com/pod-product-compliance
Lightning Source LLC
Chambersburg PA
CBHW021136300426
44113CB00006B/446